EDITORIAL TEAM
KIDS MINISTRY PUBLISHING

Chuck Peters
Director, Kids Ministry

Jeremy Carroll
Publishing Manager,
VBS and Kids Discipleship

Rhonda VanCleave
Publishing Team Leader

Debbie Miller
Writer; Serves in Children's Ministry
in Bartlesville, OK

Sara Lansford
Content Editor

Rachel Woodruff
Production Editor

Gordon Brown
Graphic Designer

Send questions/co
VBS Publishing Te
rhonda.vancleave

or by mail to
VBS Publishing T
VBS 2024 Babies
200 Powell Place, Suite 100
Brentwood, TN 37027-7707

or make comments on the web at
www.lifeway.com.

Printed in the United States of America
© 2023 Lifeway Press®

No part of this work may be reproduced or transmitted in any form or by any means, electronic or mechanical, including photocopying and recording, or by any information storage or retrieval system, except as may be expressly permitted in writing by the publisher. Requests for permission should be addressed in writing to:

Lifeway Press
200 Powell Place, Suite 100
Brentwood, TN 37027-7707.

ISBN: 9781430090175
Item: 005846943

We believe that the Bible has God for its author; salvation for its end; and truth, without any mixture of error, for its matter; and that all Scripture is totally true and trustworthy. To review Lifeway's doctrinal guideline, please visit www.lifeway.com/doctrinalguideline.

Unless otherwise indicated, all Scripture quotations are taken from the Christian Standard Bible®, Copyright © 2017 by Holman Bible Publishers. Used by permission. Christian Standard Bible® and CSB® are federally registered trademarks of Holman Bible Publishers.

Breaker Rock Beach® and any other trademarks, service marks, logos, and graphics used herein are the trademarks or registered trademarks or service marks of Lifeway. Other trademarks, service marks, graphics, and logos used in connection with this product may be the trademarks of their respective owners. You are granted no right or license with respect to any of the trademarks or service marks mentioned above or any use of such trademarks or service marks except as specifically stated within this product.

VBS 2024

LEADER TIPS

1. Familiarize yourself with the contents of this guide, the *VBS 2024 Babies–2s Leader Pack* (9781430090182), the *VBS 2024 Music for Babies–2s CD* (included in the leader pack), and the *VBS 2024 Keepsake Book* (9781430090151).
2. Print the following items to help with planning and preparation: "Planning Chart" (one per teacher), "Child Information Sheet" (one per child), "Parent Update" (one per family), "Hygiene Tips," and "Allergy Alert." (See information below.)
3. Prepare all leader pack items according to the instructions on each item.
4. Embrace the fact that you are more than a babysitter! The activities in this book are specially designed to help infants through younger 3s learn about God. Choose a few activities to do each day. Don't feel like you need to prepare twenty activities a day to fill the time. Simply choose a few and repeat them throughout the day. Put some away for a while and when you get them back out later, they will be like new to the children. It's even OK to repeat activities throughout the week—kids LOVE repetition!

SAMPLE DAILY SCHEDULE*

• Activities	80 minutes
• Recreation	20 minutes
• Snack	20 minutes
• Rest Time	30 minutes
• Repeated Activities and Departure	30 minutes

*For young babies, the daily schedule is determined by the needs of each baby. Feeding, diapering, and meeting basic needs are the top priorities.

AUDIO RESOURCES

You can find audio resources on the *VBS 2024 Music for Babies–2s CD* in the leader pack or purchase them for download at www.lifeway.com.

PRINTABLE RESOURCES

These printable teacher helps can be downloaded in the Helps section at https://vbs.lifeway.com by clicking on the resources tab.

- Babies—2s Planning Chart
- Child Information Sheet
- Parent Update
- Hygiene Tips
- Allergy Alert
- Hygiene Poster—Changing Diapers
- Cleaning Poster
- Hygiene Poster—Washing Hands
- Sharing God's Plan with Parents

SAFETY AND SECURITY TIPS

- Familiarize yourself with your church's policies and observe all safety and security procedures.

- Conduct background screenings and check references of every volunteer prior to participating in VBS. (Screening procedures for teachers in kids ministry may be found at www.lifeway.com/backgroundchecks.)

- Maintain appropriate leader/child ratios (1 leader for every 3 children, with a maximum enrollment of 12, including leaders). Ensure at least 2 leaders are with children at all times.

- Remove all potential safety and choking hazards from the room. Watch for sharp edges, protruding bolts, and loose items small enough to fit through a paper towel tube (anything that fits is a choking hazard). Cover outlets with safety plugs. Install safety latches on cabinets. Place all cords (including electrical cords and blinds) out of reach. Sit on the floor to get a child's-eye view of the room.

- Display the "Allergy Alert" outside the room for parents. Each day, list everything kids will touch, smell, or taste.

- Follow your church's sign-in procedures as parents drop off their children. Obtain a completed "Child Information Sheet" and an emergency number from parents. Pass along any special/allergy information to other leaders.

- Greet and receive children at the door. For smoother transitions and the security of children already in the room, allow only leaders and children to enter the room.

- When provided by parents in the child's diaper bag, use only those foods, diapers, wipes, and other supplies.

- Do not leave a baby unattended on a changing table or in a crib with the rails down.

- Place babies on their backs to sleep unless directed otherwise by a parent.

- Assign one leader to every two or three children if the group must leave the room. Insist that children hold the leaders' hands when traveling to a new location. Keep an accurate daily attendance list with you as you travel to make sure everyone is accounted for at all times.

HYGIENE AND SNACK TIPS

❏ Review guidelines for changing diapers, washing hands, cleaning, and disinfecting on "Hygiene Tips."

❏ Post the "Hygiene Poster—Changing Diapers" above changing tables for easy reference by leaders.

❏ Post the recipe for disinfecting solution above the sink: 4 cups water + 1 tablespoon chlorine bleach.

❏ Prepare fresh disinfecting solution each day. Pour it into a spray bottle (clearly labeled) for easy cleaning of toys and cribs. Keep out of reach of children. Display the "Cleaning Poster" for easy reference by leaders.

❏ Clean toys after each use. Every time a child touches or mouths a toy, remove it from the play area until it is cleaned. Wash toys in a dishpan of warm, soapy water; spray them with the disinfecting solution; and rinse them in clear water. Allow toys to air-dry.

❏ Wash hands vigorously for at least 20 seconds before feeding a child, before and after treating a cut, after assisting a child with toileting, and after wiping a child's nose or mouth (or your own).

❏ Post the "Washing Hands Poster" near the sink as a reminder for teachers.

❏ Clean cribs before and after the first session and after each subsequent session. Wipe crib rails, sides, and mattresses with warm, soapy water and spray with disinfecting solution. When dry, put clean sheets on the mattresses.

❏ Use caution when allowing children to taste foods approved by (but not provided by) their parents. The following foods should be avoided as choking hazards or potential allergens:

- Apples (unless peeled and cut into wafer-thin slices)
- Grapes (can block a child's upper airway when served whole)
- Hard candy and "gummy" candy
- Hot dogs
- Marshmallows
- Nuts (a common allergen)
- Oranges (seeds and pulp can present choking hazards)
- Peanut butter (a common allergen)
- Popcorn
- Pretzels
- Raisins
- Sunflower and watermelon seeds

OVERVIEW OF BIBLE STORIES

Bible Verse: Thank You, God, for Jesus. *Luke 2:38*

DAY 1	DAY 2	DAY 3	DAY 4	DAY 5
Bible Story	**Bible Story**	**Bible Story**	**Bible Story**	**Bible Story**
Ruth's Family	Samuel Helped at the Temple (Church)	God Chose David to Become King	Simeon and Anna Saw Baby Jesus	Jesus Went to the Temple (Church)
Ruth 1:22; 2:1-23; 4:13-17	*1 Samuel 1:20-28; 2:11,18-21,26; 3:1-2,15,19*	*1 Samuel 16*	*Luke 2:21-40*	*Luke 2:40-52*
Today's Point	**Today's Point:**	**Today's Point:**	**Today's Point:**	**Today's Point:**
God will take care of me.	People at church teach me about God.	God has a plan for me.	I can thank God for Jesus.	I can learn about God at church.

CHRIST CONNECTION

Jesus came to earth to do God's plan.

LEVEL OF BIBLICAL LEARNING: PEOPLE

God has a plan for me.

The Levels of Biblical Learning is a tool that reflects levels of understanding at each age that follow how God designed children to learn. For more information visit www.lifeway.com/lobl.

BIBLE CONTENT

WHAT IS BIBLE STORY PLUS?

Bible Story Plus is a short "group time" type experience for older 2s and younger 3s. It may not occur as a scheduled activity time each day. Instead, it may happen more naturally as you sit on the floor and several children join you of their own accord. This may mean you do Bible Story Plus more than once during the day.

Keep in mind the attention span of the preschoolers in your room and keep group activities short and active. Encourage everyone to join you in the activity, but understand that some children may be ready to move on more quickly than others. It is OK for a child to move to another activity in the room while you continue Bible Story Plus with other children.

BIBLE STORY PLUS MAY INCLUDE …

Telling the Bible Story

Singing or Moving to Music

Playing a Game

Joining in a group activity with friends

DAY 1

RUTH'S FAMILY

Theme Verse: Thank You, God, for Jesus. *Luke 2:38*

Today's Point: God will take care of me.

BABIES–YOUNGER 1s

—Based on Ruth 1:22; 2:1-23; 4:13-17

- Ruth and Naomi moved to Bethlehem.
- They needed food to eat.
- Ruth found a field where workers were cutting grain.
- Ruth worked hard to pick up grain.
- Boaz told Ruth she could have the grain.
- Boaz was kind to Ruth.
- Boaz and Ruth were married.
- Boaz and Ruth had a baby boy and named him Obed.

OLDER 1s–2s

—Based on Ruth 1:22; 2:1-23; 4:13-17

Ruth and Naomi had just moved to the town of Bethlehem. They needed food to eat. Ruth said to Naomi, "Let me go to the grain fields. I'll pick up the grain that is left by the workers." Ruth found a field where workers were cutting grain. She worked hard to pick up grain.

Boaz was the owner of the field. He saw Ruth and asked, "Who is that woman?" The man in charge of the workers said, "She and Naomi just moved here. She asked if she could pick up the leftover grain."

Boaz called to Ruth, "Stay with my workers. Pick up the grain that is left. When you are thirsty, get a drink from the water jars." Boaz invited Ruth to eat with his workers. After eating, Ruth went back to the field to pick up grain. Ruth told Naomi about Boaz and how kind he had been to her.

Ruth worked in Boaz's field every day until all the grain was gathered. Later Boaz and Ruth were married. After a while, they had a baby boy. They named him Obed.

BIBLE STORY PLUS

Supplies: Bible, "Bible Story Picture 1" (pack item 1), "Families" (pack item 12), muffin pan, ball pit balls

- Place family picture circles from "Families" (pack item 12) in the bottom of half of the muffin cups.
- Cover all the muffin cups with a ball except one.
- Sit on the floor with the pan in front of you and invite children to play a game.
- Tell the children you are looking for pictures of families. Pick up a ball and encourage the children to look for a picture.
- Place the ball in the empty spot and remove the picture if there is one.
- Suggest another child pick up a ball looking for a picture.
- Each time you pick up a ball, move it to the empty spot.
- Set the muffin pan aside when all pictures have been found.
- Show "Bible Story Picture 1" (pack item 1). Point to Ruth.
- Open the Bible to Ruth and tell the story.
- Comment: "God had a plan for Ruth's family. He took care of Ruth, and He will take care of you."

FIND A HIDDEN BIBLE

Supplies: Bible, small baby blanket;
EXTEND: "Bible Match" (pack item 10)

- Sit on the floor with an infant in your lap.
- Lay the Bible on the floor in front of you and cover it with the blanket.
- Say: "Where is the Bible?"
- Guide the infant to pull the blanket off the Bible.
- Act surprised when the Bible is uncovered. Cover the Bible and play again.
- Place your hand over her hand and guide her in opening the Bible to the book of Ruth.
- Point to the words and tell the Bible story.
- Say: "Thank You, God, for taking care of Ruth and her family."
- Cover the Bible. Play as long as the baby is interested.

EXTEND: Guide older infants in matching a pair of Bible cards using "Bible Match" (pack item 10).

SNACK ON ROUND CEREAL

Supplies: "Bible Story Picture 1" (pack item 1), "Grain Cards" (pack item 14), clear contact plastic, O-shaped oat cereal, "Allergy Alert" (printable resource, see page 2 for instructions), high chair with tray

- Cover "Grain Cards" (pack item 14) with a sheet of clear contact plastic.
- Lay one set of the cards on a high chair tray. Seat an infant in the high chair and drop a few pieces of O-shaped cereal on the tray.
- Point to and describe the pictures of grain as the infant eats the oat cereal.
- Show "Bible Story Picture 1" (pack item 1). Say: "God had a plan for Ruth and her family."
- Open the Bible and share the Bible story.
- Sing "God Has a Plan for Me" (Music and Movement Tab).

DAY 1   7   BABIES–YOUNGER 1s • BIBLE ACTIVITIES

SCOOP GRAIN

Supplies: Bible, "Bible Story Picture 1" (pack item 1), tub, scoops, grain, vinyl tablecloth, "Allergy Alert" (printable resource, see page 2 for instructions)

- Place "Bible Story Picture 1" (pack item 1) in the bottom of a tub and cover it with grain.
- Spread tablecloth on the floor; set the tub in the middle.
- Hand a scoop to a child and suggest he scoop grain and pour it back into the tub.
- Talk about the grain and what kinds of food are made from grain.
- Move some of the grain aside and help the child pull the picture out of the tub.
- Point to the grain in the picture and tell the child that Ruth needed grain for food.
- Guide the child to open the Bible to Ruth. Tell the Bible story in your own words.
- Say: "Thank You, God, for taking care of Ruth's family."

PLAY A MATCHING GAME

Supplies: "Grain Cards" (pack item 14), "Allergy Alert" (printable resource, see page 2 for instructions), O-shaped oat cereal, napkins

- Pour several pieces of cereal on a napkin and invite a child to enjoy a snack.

- Show him the grain cards, describing each picture.
- Guide him to match the cards. Remind him that God had a plan for Ruth's family.

EXTEND: Use only two sets of matching cards with younger preschoolers and challenge older preschoolers to match all four sets. Older preschoolers can play a game of memory using the cards.

FOLD BABY BLANKETS

Supplies: Bible, 2–3 baby blankets, basket

- Place the Bible in the bottom of the basket and lay the unfolded blankets on top.
- Set the basket on the floor and invite a child to help you fold the blankets.
- Show the child how to fold one of the blankets and set it aside.
- Assist the child as needed in folding the remaining blankets. Talk about ways families take care of babies.
- Remove the Bible from the basket and guide the child to open it to Ruth. Share the Bible story in your own words.
- Comment: "Ruth and Boaz had a baby boy. God had a plan for Ruth and her family, and He took care of them."
- Sing "God Has a Plan for Me" (Music and Movement Tab).

DAY 1   8   OLDER 1s–2s • BIBLE ACTIVITIES

DAY 2

SAMUEL HELPED AT THE TEMPLE (CHURCH)

Theme Verse: Thank You, God, for Jesus. *Luke 2:38*

Today's Point: People at church teach me about God.

BABIES–YOUNGER 1s

—*Based on 1 Samuel 1:20-28; 2:11,18-21,26; 3:1-2,15,19*

- Hannah had a baby boy named Samuel.
- Samuel went to church with his mother and father.
- Eli was a teacher at the church.
- Samuel became Eli's helper at church.
- Eli taught Samuel about God.
- As Samuel grew, he learned more and more about God.

OLDER 1s–2s

—*Based on 1 Samuel 1:20-28; 2:11,18-21,26; 3:1-2,15,19*

Hannah had a baby boy and named him Samuel. When he was a little boy, Samuel went with his mother and father to the temple (church).

Eli was a teacher at the temple (church). Hannah wanted Samuel to be Eli's helper at the temple (church). Eli could teach Samuel about God.

Samuel was a good helper for Eli. Every morning Samuel would open the doors to the temple (church). Samuel listened to Eli and did those things Eli told him to do.

As Samuel grew, he kept helping Eli. Eli kept teaching Samuel about God. Samuel learned more and more about God.

BIBLE STORY PLUS

Supplies: Bible, "Bible Story Picture 2" (pack item 2), "Bible Marker" (pack item 6)

- Place a "Bible Marker" (pack item 6) in your Bible at 1 Samuel.
- Invite children to join you in a circle.
- Sing "This Is The Way" (Music and Movement Tab). End the song by singing, "This is the way we sit on the floor."
- Show the "Bible Story Picture 2" (pack item 2) and encourage children to tell you what they see.
- Invite a child to open the Bible to the marker in 1 Samuel. Tell the Bible story.
- Comment: "God had a plan for Samuel to learn about Him at church. People at church teach you about God too."
- Say a prayer thanking God for people who teach us at church.

ROCK AND READ WITH A LEADER

Supplies: Bible, "Book: *God Has a Plan for Me*" (pack item 21)

- Sit in a rocking chair with an infant in your lap.
- Read "Book: *God Has a Plan for Me*" (pack item 21).
- Turn back and look at the picture of Samuel. Say: "We can read the story about Samuel in the Bible."
- Open the Bible to 1 Samuel and share the Bible story.
- Continue: "God had a plan for Samuel. God has a plan for you." Rock and sing "God Has a Plan for Me" (Music and Movement Tab).

PLAY WITH TOY PEOPLE FIGURES

Supplies: "Bible Story Picture 2" (pack item 2), toy people figures, tub of plastic blocks

- Place the "Bible Story Picture 2" (pack item 2) in the bottom of the tub of blocks.
- Bury the toy people figures in the tub of blocks.
- Sit on the floor with a baby on your lap.
- Guide the child to play with the blocks. Show him how to snap the blocks together.
- Remove the Bible story picture from the tub and briefly tell the story.
- Help him find the people figures hiding in the blocks.
- Talk about people who teach him about God.
- Say a prayer thanking God for leaders and parents who teach him about God.

READ ON A BEACH TOWEL

Supplies: Bible, "Book: *God Has a Plan for Me*" (pack item 21), Keepsake Book, beach towel

- Spread a beach towel on the floor in a quiet area.
- Lay the Bible, "Book: *God Has a Plan for Me*" (pack item 21), and a Keepsake Book on the towel.
- Encourage a child to sit on the towel and read with you. Look at the Keepsake Book together.
- Show her the "Bible Story Picture 2" (pack item 2) and name the people in the picture. *(Eli and Samuel)*
- Assist her in opening the Bible to 1 Samuel and tell the Bible story in your own words.
- Say a brief prayer thanking God for people who teach at church.

HELP AT CHURCH

Supplies: "Bible Story Picture 2" (pack item 2), painter's tape, spray bottle, water, rag; EXTEND: *VBS 2024 Theme Stickers* (9781430088820)

- Tape "Bible Story Picture 2" (pack item 2) to the wall at child's eye level.
- Pour a small amount of water in the spray bottle.
- Show a child how to spray water on a table and wipe it up with the rag.
- Point to the picture and tell the story about Samuel.
- Sing "This Is the Way" (Music and Movement Tab). Substitute the word *clean* for the beach words.

 EXTEND: Use theme stickers to add seashells and animals to page 7 in Keepsake Books.

PLAY A MISSING OBJECT GAME

Supplies: Bible, cup, block, toy people figure, rhythm instrument, tray

- Place the items on the tray and set the tray on a low table.
- Invite a child to sit at the table and play a game with you.
- Point to and label each item on the tray. Talk about how each of the items is used at VBS.
- Tell the child to close his eyes. Remove one object from the tray.
- Say: "Open your eyes and tell me what is missing." Give the child time to look at all the objects. Give hints if he has trouble guessing the missing item.
- Play until only one object is remaining.
- Guide the child to open the Bible to 1 Samuel. Tell the Bible story. Talk about how you are learning about God at church just like Samuel.

DAY 2 — 12 — OLDER 1s–2s • BIBLE ACTIVITIES

DAY 3 — GOD CHOSE DAVID TO BECOME KING

Theme Verse: Thank You, God, for Jesus. *Luke 2:38*

Today's Point: God has a plan for me.

BABIES–YOUNGER 1s

—Based on 1 Samuel 16

- God told Samuel to go to Jesse's house in Bethlehem.
- God said He had chosen one of Jesse's sons to be the new king.
- Samuel saw seven of Jesse's sons, but none of them was the one God chose.
- Jesse's youngest son, David, came to Samuel.
- God told Samuel that David would be the next king.
- Samuel let David's family know that David would be the new king.

OLDER 1s–2s

—Based on 1 Samuel 16

Samuel was a prophet. One day God spoke to Samuel. "Go to Jesse's house in Bethlehem. I have chosen one of his sons as the new king."

Samuel traveled to Bethlehem.

Samuel saw Jesse's oldest son. He thought that this son was the new king. But God said, "He is not the one."

Samuel looked at seven of Jesse's sons. He said, "God has not chosen any of these. Are these all your sons?"

Jesse said, "My youngest son, David, is taking care of the sheep."

Samuel said, "Send for him."

David came to Samuel. God said, "Anoint him. He is the one."

Samuel poured some oil on David. David would be the next king.

BIBLE STORY PLUS

Supplies: Bible, "Bible Story Picture 3" (pack item 3), crown, "Bible Times Clothes Instructions" (pack item 26), fabric, fabric scissors

- Follow the instructions on "Bible Times Clothes Instructions" (pack item 26) to make a Bible times outfit.
- Gather children and invite them to take turns dressing in a Bible times outfit and wearing the crown.
- Gather the crown and clothes and set them aside. Sit in a circle with the children and show "Bible Story Picture 3" (pack item 3). Remind boys and girls that David took care of his father's sheep before he became the king.
- Open the Bible to 1 Samuel 16 and tell the Bible story.
- Comment: "God had a plan for David when he was a boy. God planned for him to be a king."

EXTEND: Take pictures of each child who dresses like a king and add to pages 14 or 15 in the Keepsake Books.

STACK BLOCKS

Supplies: Bible, "Stand-up Figures" (pack item 7), blocks, clear contact plastic, tape

- Cover "Stand-up Figures" (pack item 7) in clear contact plastic for durability.
- Attach the figures of boy David and the sheep to blocks.
- Sit on the floor with an infant on your lap or seated in front of you.
- Describe the blocks and talk about the colors. Help him stack the blocks.
- Find the blocks with David and the sheep. Line the blocks up.
- Say: "David took care of sheep."
- Show "Bible Story Picture 3" (pack item 3) and point to David. Open the Bible to 1 Samuel 16 and tell the story.

Leader Tip: Help a younger infant stack blocks by placing your hand over his hand.

DROP LIDS IN A CONTAINER

Supplies: "Families" (pack item 12), canning lid flats, clear packing tape, clean oatmeal container, colored contact plastic

- Cover the container with colored contact plastic.
- Use wide tape to attach the family picture circles from "Families" (pack item 12) to canning lid flats. Be sure to use all the Bible story family pictures along with some of the modern family pictures.
- Sit with an infant in your lap. Show him how to drop the lids in the oatmeal container. Infants can grab items easier than they can release. Young infants will need more help.
- Talk about the families on the lids. Find the lid with David's family. Comment: "David was a shepherd boy. He helped his family take care of sheep. God had a plan for David to be a king."
- Continue to drop lids in the box and talk about families.
- Say a prayer thanking God that He has a plan for each of us.

Leader Tip: Challenge older infants by cutting a slit in the lid of the oatmeal container to drop the lids through.

DAY 3

BABIES–YOUNGER 1s • BIBLE ACTIVITIES

FOLLOW A PATH

Supplies: Bible, "Bible Story Picture 3" (pack item 3), brown paper, marker, tape

- Trace a pair of shoes on several sheets of brown paper and cut out the prints.
- Tape prints to the floor to create a path. Lay the Bible and "Bible Story Picture 3" (pack item 3) at the end of the path.
- Help a child follow the path by stepping on the shoe prints.
- Sit with her at the end of the path and look at "Bible Story Picture 3" (pack item 3). Talk about the people in the picture.
- Open the Bible to 1 Samuel 16 and tell the Bible story.
- Say: "God had a plan for David. He has a plan for you."
- Encourage her to walk along the path and repeat, "God has a plan for me."

PLAY WITH STAND-UP FIGURES

Supplies: "Stand-up Figures" (pack item 7), blocks, animal figure toys, cardboard tubes

- Attach the stand-up figures to cardboard tubes and place them in a basket. Arrange the blocks and animals on a mat.

- Join a child who has begun to explore the blocks and animals.
- Set the basket of figures on the mat. Help the child stand the figures among the blocks.
- Say: "God sent Samuel to find David. God had a plan for David to be a king."
- Use the figures to tell the story of David.

MATCH FAMILY PICTURES

Supplies: "Families" (pack item 12), sticky notes, painter's tape

- Choose six pairs of family circles, including David's family.
- Tape the circles to the wall in a mixed-up order.
- Show a child the pictures of families on the wall. Look for matching pairs of families.
- Invite her to help you cover each circle with a sticky note.
- Encourage her to find the matching families by lifting the sticky notes. Remove sticky notes when a match is found.
- Point to the picture of David's family. Tell the Bible story. Comment: "God had a plan for David to be a king."

Leader Tip: Choose only three matching families for younger preschoolers.

DAY 4 — SIMEON AND ANNA SAW BABY JESUS

Theme Verse: Thank You, God, for Jesus. *Luke 2:38*

Today's Point: I can thank God for Jesus.

BABIES–YOUNGER 1s

—Based on Luke 2:21-40

- Mary and Joseph took Baby Jesus to church.
- Mary and Joseph met a man named Simeon.
- Simeon held Baby Jesus in his arms.
- Simeon thanked God for Baby Jesus.
- Anna saw Baby Jesus and His family.
- Anna thanked God for sending Jesus.
- Joseph and Mary took Baby Jesus home.
- Jesus learned and grew every day with His family.

BIBLE STORY FOR 2s

—Based on Luke 2:21-40

Mary and Joseph took Baby Jesus to the temple (church).

When Mary, Joseph, and Jesus went to the temple (church), they met a man named Simeon. Simeon held Baby Jesus in his arms. Simeon was happy to see Jesus! Simeon thanked God for Baby Jesus.

Anna was also at the temple (church) that day. When Anna saw Mary, Joseph, and Baby Jesus, she thanked God for sending Jesus.

Joseph and Mary took Baby Jesus home. Jesus learned and grew every day with His family.

BIBLE STORY PLUS

Supplies: Bible, "Bible Story Picture 4" (pack item 4), "Bible Marker" (pack item 6), baby doll, baby blanket, rhythm instruments, Music for Babies—2s CD

- Place a "Bible Marker" (pack item 6) in your Bible at Luke 2.
- Invite children to sit on the floor with you and play instruments. Play and sing "Church."
- Gather the instruments and set aside. Spread the blanket on the floor and place the doll on the blanket. Wrap the baby doll in the blanket and lay it in your lap.
- Show "Bible Story Picture 4" and talk about the people in the picture.
- Say: "Mary and Joseph took Baby Jesus to church." Remind the children that their parents or grown-ups bring them to church too.
- Hand the picture to a child to hold. Open the Bible to Luke 2 and tell the Bible story. Remove the marker and read the verse.
- Guide the children to pass the doll around the circle saying, "Thank You, God, for Jesus" before passing the doll to the next person.

ROLL A BALL

Supplies: Bible, "Bible Marker" (pack item 6), ball, Music for Babies–2s CD

- Place the "Bible Marker" (pack item 6) at Luke 2.
- Sit on the floor with a baby. Place your hand over his and open the Bible to the marker in Luke 2.
- Point to the words and read the verse.
- Turn him so he is facing you and help him roll the ball back and forth to you.
- Play and sing "Jesus Is Born" as you roll the ball.

Leader Tip: Guide older infants in rolling the ball to a friend while you sing.

SHAKE BABY RATTLES AND MOVE ABOUT THE ROOM

Supplies: "Bible Story Picture 4" (pack item 4), baby rattles, painter's tape

- Tape "Bible Story Picture 4" (pack item 4) to the wall.
- Pick up an infant and show him how to shake a baby rattle. Assist him by placing your hand over his and shaking the rattle.
- Move about the room, shaking the rattle and repeating the verse, "Thank You, God, for Jesus."
- Stop in front of the picture. Point to the people in the picture. Comment: "Mary and Joseph took Baby Jesus to church. Simeon and Anna both thanked God for Jesus. I am glad your parents or grown-ups bring you to church. Thank You, God, for Jesus and thank You, God for (child's name)."
- Sit or lay the infant on the floor and hand him the rattle to play.

CARE FOR A DOLL

Supplies: Bible, baby doll, small diaper bag, baby bottle, rattle, blanket, other baby items

- Fill the diaper bag with the items. Lay the doll and the diaper bag on a mat.
- Invite a child to sit on the floor with you. Encourage him to open the diaper bag. Identify and talk about each item he finds in the bag.
- Say: "Mommies and daddies use these things to take care of their babies. Your parents take care of you." Talk about the things his parents do for him.
- Open the Bible to Luke 2. Comment: "Mary and Joseph were Jesus' parents. They took care of Him, and they took Him to church."
- Point to the words and share the Bible story. Say a simple prayer thanking God for Jesus.
- Allow the child to continue to play with the doll.

PLAY WITH PEOPLE FIGURES

Supplies: Bible, toy people figures, blocks

- Sit on the floor and invite a child to join you in building a church. Add the people figures to the church building and talk about families taking their children to church.

- Guide the child to open the Bible to Luke. Point to the words in Luke 2 and share the Bible story.
- Comment: "Jesus' parents took Him to church. Simeon thanked God for Baby Jesus. We can thank God too."
- Sing "Thank You, God" (Music and Movement Tab).

ROLL INFLATABLE CUBE AND SING

Supplies: "Inflatable Cube Inserts" (pack item 28), *Giant Inflatable Game Cube* (9781087779812) (If an inflatable cube is not available, a box can be substituted. Tape a sheet protector to each side of the box and insert the cards.)

- Place the "Inflatable Cube Inserts" (pack item 28) in the pockets of the inflatable cube.
- Show a child how to roll the cube. When the cube stops, point to the card on the top and sing the song.
- Roll the cube again and sing a new song.
- Point to the insert, "Thank You, God," and sing this song if it hasn't already been sung. Comment: "We are learning about Jesus and His family today. Thank You, God, for Jesus."
- Sing more songs if the child is interested.

DAY 4   OLDER 1s–2s • BIBLE ACTIVITIES

DAY 5 — JESUS WENT TO THE TEMPLE (CHURCH)

Theme Verse: Thank You, God, for Jesus. *Luke 2:38*

Today's Point: I can learn about God at church.

BABIES–YOUNGER 1s

—*Based on Luke 2:40-52*

- Jesus went to church with His family.
- When it was time to go home, Mary and Joseph could not find Jesus.
- Mary and Joseph found Jesus in the church.
- Jesus was listening and talking to the teachers.
- Jesus told Mary He was at the church talking about God.
- Jesus went home with Mary and Joseph.

OLDER 1s–2s

—*Based on Luke 2:40-52*

When Jesus was 12 years old, He went to the temple (church).

After everyone left Jerusalem, Mary and Joseph could not find Jesus.

Mary and Joseph hurried back to look for Jesus. They found Jesus in the temple (church). He was listening to the teachers and asking them questions.

Mary asked Jesus, "Why are You here? We have been looking for You everywhere."

Jesus answered, "Didn't you know I would be in the temple (church) talking about God?"

Jesus went home with Mary and Joseph.

BIBLE STORY PLUS

Supplies: 3–4 Bibles, "Bible Story Picture 5" (pack item 5), "Bible Markers" (pack item 6) "Bible Match" (pack item 10)

- Insert a "Bible Marker" (pack item 6) at Luke 2:38 in each Bible.
- Arrange the Bibles on the floor. Talk about and compare the colors and sizes.
- Encourage children to open Bibles to the verse markers at Luke 2:38. Point to the words and repeat the verse, "Thank You, God, for Jesus."
- Lay one set of the "Bible Match" (pack item 10) cards on the floor. Talk about these Bibles. Say that when Jesus went to the temple, their Bible was a scroll. Remind children that a temple is a church.
- Show one card from the matching set and ask which Bible it matches. Match the remaining cards one at a time.
- Pick up a Bible and share the Bible story.
- Say a brief prayer thanking God for Jesus and that we can read about Him in the Bible.

PLAY WITH POP BEADS

Supplies: "Bible Story Picture 5" (pack item 5), tub, large pop beads, Music for Babies–2s CD

- Place the "Bible Story Picture 5" (pack item 5) in the bottom of the tub.
- Add the pop beads on top of the picture.
- Sit on the floor with a baby on your lap. Help her snap the beads together.
- Pull out the Bible story picture. Point to and identify the people in the picture. Say: "Joseph and Mary were Jesus' parents. One day they could not find Jesus."
- Share the Bible story in your own words.
- Comment: "I am happy you come to church to learn about Jesus. God has a plan for you."
- Say a prayer thanking God for Jesus and for people who teach us about Jesus.
- Sing "Learn About God."

EXPLORE A MOBILE

Supplies: "Families" (pack item 12), "Bible Match" (pack item 10), embroidery hoop, bright-colored ribbon, tape, Music for Babies–2s CD

- Tie several ribbons onto the embroidery hoop. Make a mobile by taping four "Bible Match" (pack item 10) cards and one "Families" (pack item 12) circle of each Bible story to the ribbons.
- Hang the hoop from the ceiling.
- Hold an infant up to see the pictures and touch the ribbons.
- Point to Jesus and His parents as you tell the Bible story.
- Sing "Jesus Taught."

DAY 5   BABIES–YOUNGER 1s • BIBLE ACTIVITIES

MAKE A COLLAGE ON A CHURCH SHAPE

Supplies: Bible, "Bible Story Picture 5" (pack item 5), cardboard, glue, small plate, foam paintbrush, scrapbook paper scraps, tablecloth, scissors

- Cover the table with a tablecloth. Pour glue in a small plate and stir in a few drops of water.
- Cut a simple church shape out of cardboard.
- Demonstrate how to use the paintbrush to cover the church with glue and then scraps of paper.
- Paint glue over the top of the paper to seal the collage.
- Talk to the child about church. Say: "This shape reminds me of a church. When Jesus was a boy, His parents found Him listening to teachers at the church."
- Open the Bible and share the Bible story. Say a simple prayer thanking God for Jesus.

MOVE PAINT IN A BAG

Supplies: Bible, "Bible Story Picture 5" (pack item 5), 2-gallon ziplock bag, heavy tape, tempera paint (Tempera paint is sometimes egg based. Consider posting an "Allergy Alert.")

- Place approximately a half a cup of tempera paint in the bag. Remove the air as you seal the bag.
- Lay "Bible Story Picture 5" (pack item 5) on the table and place the bag of paint on top. Tape the bag to the table.
- Guide a child in moving the paint around in the bag.
- Help her find Jesus in the picture. Talk about the Bible story as you work.

DRESS IN BIBLE TIMES CLOTHES

Supplies: Bible, Keepsake Book, tape, "Bible Times Clothes Instructions" (pack item 26), sandals, Music for Babies–2s CD

- Prepare clothes as described in "Bible Times Clothes Instructions" (pack item 26).
- Tape a path around the room. Place the Bible and Keepsake Book at the end of the path.
- Invite a child to try on the clothes and sandals.
- Guide the child to walk on the path. Tell him Mary and Joseph walked to find Jesus. Sit at the end of the path.
- Open the Keepsake Book to page 10 and look at picture of boy Jesus in the temple. Open the Bible to Luke 2.
- Say: "This is where we read the story about Mary and Joseph looking for Jesus." Tell the Bible story in your own words.
- Sing "Jesus Loves You and Me."

WHAT ARE THEME ACTIVITIES?

The activities in this section of the book relate to the overall theme and Bible content of VBS. Unlike the previous "Bible activities," theme activities do not necessarily relate to a specific Bible story. But they're not "just for fun." They are still designed to help you teach Bible truths in ways that are meaningful and applicable to young children. Choose 2–3 of these activities to use in addition to the Bible activities each day. You may choose to use different activities each day or repeat activities throughout the week of VBS. It's totally up to you! Each page is labeled across the bottom to help you know which activities are designed for babies—younger 1s and which are for older 1s–2s.

LOOKING FOR RECREATION IDEAS FOR OLDER 2s?

Check out the other side of this page!

THIS ICON INDICATES THAT AN ACTIVITY USES THE

VBS 2024 KEEPSAKE BOOK (9781430090151). This book makes a great souvenir from the week! Ideas for using the Keepsake Book are available on the inside back cover of this book.

THEME ACTIVITIES

RECREATION IDEAS

Fill a Picnic Basket
Supplies: picnic basket; plastic fruit; plastic sandwich box; empty juice box; empty, small, round chip container

- Sit the children in a circle. Place the picnic basket on the floor in front of one child. Hand an item to the child next to the basket and guide the children to pass the item around the circle until it reaches the basket. Once they understand how to pass the item, hand the child a second item to pass. Keep handing items until all items are making their way around the circle to the basket. Cheer the children on as they work. Vary the activity for older toddlers by sitting them in a line facing forward and passing items from the back to the front.

Animal Stomp
Supplies: none

- Name a Breaker Rock Beach animal.
- Demonstrate how the animal moves.
- Encourage children to move like the animal.
- Challenge older children to name an animal and demonstrate how it moves.

Other Quick Ideas

- Drive pretend beach vehicles around the room or down the hall, making beep noises.
- Watch and chase bubbles.
- Go on a hike around the building to look for Breaker Rock Beach decorations. Use wrapping paper tubes as walking sticks.
- Play with a parachute, tossing sponges up and down pretending they are salmon.

Hit a Beach Ball
Supplies: beach ball, string

- Inflate a beach ball and hang it from the ceiling. Hang it low enough for a toddler to be able to hit the ball.
- Stand in a circle and show children how to hit the ball. Help a toddler by placing your hand over his and hit the ball.
- Use a binder clip or clothespin to pull the string up higher and clip the ball out of the way when the game is over.

Breaker Rock Beach Obstacle Course
Supplies: small beach chair, sand pail, beach towel, small tent, vehicle made using "Vehicle Wheel and Instructions" (pack item 29 and "Vehicle Front" (pack item 30), other beach items

- Use the items to create an obstacle course. Demonstrate how to move through the course. Walk around the chair, hop over a rolled-up beach towel, move in and out of the tent, and so forth. Help younger toddlers by holding their hands through the course. Encourage older toddlers to move through on their own. Rearrange the course and try again.

EXAMINE ROCKS AND PEBBLES

Supplies: "Bible Markers" (pack item 6), tape or glue, small rocks, pebbles, empty plastic jar with lid

- Place several rocks and pebbles in a jar and secure the lid with tape or glue.
- Tape a "Bible Marker" (pack item 6) to one side of the jar.
- Sit with a child in your lap. Shake the jar and say: "If we went to a beach, we could find rocks and pebbles."
- Point to and read the words on the verse marker.
- Demonstrate how to shake the jar and make noise.
- Assist the child in shaking the jar while you clap and chant, "Jesus, Jesus, He Loves Me" (Music and Movement tab).

PAT A MAT AND DISCOVER THE TIDE POOL

Supplies: "Under the Tide Pool" (pack item 11), gallon-size ziplock bag, heavy tape, blue or green hair gel (or blue food coloring); EXTEND: "Bible Story Picture" (pack items 1–5)

- Pour one cup of blue water or gel in a ziplock bag. Remove the air as you seal the bag.
- Lay either side of "Under the Tide Pool" (pack item 11) faceup on the table. Place the bag on top of the picture. Tape the bag to the table, taping around all four edges.
- Sit at the table with an infant on your lap. Tap the bag and comment about it moving. Encourage the infant to tap the bag.
- Point to and identify the objects in the tide pool as the infant continues to pat the bag.
- Sing "This Is the Way" (Music and Movement Tab) as the child moves the gel around in the bag.

EXTEND: Remove the picture and slide the day's Bible story picture under the bag. Examine the picture and tell the Bible story.

DAYS 1–5

LIFT-A-FLAP

Supplies: "Animal Match" (pack item 9), "Bible Match" (pack item 10), construction paper, painter's tape

- Tape a few cards from "Animal Match" (pack item 9) and "Bible Match" (pack item 10) to the wall around the room.
- Tape a half sheet of construction paper over each card. Tape across the top of the construction paper to create a flap over each of the cards.
- Pick up an infant and walk around the room. Stop each time you discover a flap. Comment: "What could be under this flap?" Guide the child to lift the flap to see an animal or Bible.
- Point to and identify the animals. Each time you see a Bible card, say the Bible verse, "Thank You, God, for Jesus."

ROLL A GAME CUBE

Supplies: "Book: *God Has a Plan for Me*" (pack item 21), "Book: *Let's Go Camping*" (pack item 23), "Bible Story Pictures" (pack items 1–5), "Bible Marker" (pack item 6), *Giant Inflatable Game Cube* (9781087779812), "Inflatable Cube Inserts" (pack item 28) (If an inflatable cube is not available, a box can be substituted. Tape a sheet protector to each side of the box and insert the cards.)

- Insert two song cards from "Inflatable Cube Inserts" (pack item 28), "Book: *God Has a Plan for Me*" (pack item 21), "Book: *Let's Go Camping*" (pack item 23), a "Bible Marker" (pack item 6), and the day's Bible story picture in the inflatable game cube pockets.
- Sit with an infant on the floor and show him how to roll the cube. When the cube stops, guide a child to choose a pocket. Talk about what is in the pocket. Say the verse, sing a song, talk about the Bible Story Picture, or read the book.
- Invite a child to roll the cube again and choose another pocket.

DAYS 1–5

PLAY WITH ANIMALS

Supplies: Bible, "Bible Markers" (pack item 6), "Flip-book: *Breaker Rock Beach*" (pack item 24), "Flip-book Assembly" (pack item 33), toy animal figures, beach towel

- Assemble the "Flip-book: *Breaker Rock Beach*" (pack item 24) according to the instructions on "Flip-book Assembly" (pack item 33).
- Mark the session Bible story with a "Bible Marker" (pack item 6).
- Seat an infant on a beach towel on the floor. Place toy animal figures on the floor in front of her.
- Allow her to explore the animals. Name and describe each animal for her.
- Show her the "Flip-book: *Breaker Rock Beach*" (pack item 24). Talk about each animal as you flip through the book. Point out when animal figures match the animals in the pictures.
- Open the Bible to the marker. Place your hand over hers and tap the page. Read the words on the marker.

Leader Tip: Lay an infant on her stomach if she is not able to sit on her own. Clean and disinfect any animal figures mouthed by infants.

MAKE TIDE POOL LIFE HANDPRINTS

Supplies: "Tide Pool Life Handprint Patterns" (pack item 34); washable red, orange, green, and brown paint; foam paintbrush; shallow pan; white paper; marker; painting smock

- Put a painting smock on the infant. Pour a small amount of paint in the shallow pan.
- Refer to "Tide Pool Life Handprint Patterns" (pack item 34) for handprint animal ideas. Sit at a table with the infant in your lap.
- Use the foam brush to apply paint to the child's hand for handprints. Name and describe the tide pool animals as you assist a child to make handprints on white paper.
- Write the child's name and *VBS 2024* in one corner.
- Say a brief prayer thanking God for fun at VBS.

EXTEND: Make crab handprints on pages 12 and 13 of the Keepsake Book and fingerprint leaves in the trees on page 3.

DAYS 1–5

EXPLORE SAND TOYS

Supplies: *VBS 2024 Sandcastle Molds* (9781430092964), sand pail, shovel, plastic tub, Music for Babies–2s CD; EXTEND: "Sand Recipes" (pack item 25), "Allergy Alert" (printable resource, see page 2 for instructions)

- Place the sand toys in a tub on the floor. Sit with an infant in your lap and set the tub of toys on the floor in front of you.
- Encourage the infant to play with the sand toys. Talk about the fun of playing with sand at the beach. Sing "Breaker Rock Beach" while children play with the toys.

EXTEND: Use "Sand Recipes" (pack item 25) to create DIY sand or moon sand for older infants. Supervise infants carefully when playing with sand.

READ IN A BEACH CHAIR

Supplies: Bible, "Book: *Let's Go Camping*" (pack item 23), "Picnic Food" (pack item 18), child-size beach chair, plastic picnic basket, clear contact plastic

- Cover the "Picnic Food" (pack item 18) with clear contact plastic. Place the food in the picnic basket.
- Put the Bible and book on the floor next to the beach chair.
- Help an infant sit in the chair. Sit on the floor next to the infant and help him remove the food from the picnic basket. Pretend to have a picnic.
- Hand him "Book: *Let's Go Camping*" (pack item 23). Help him turn the pages and look at the pictures while you read.
- Open the Bible and tell the Bible story.

DAYS 1–5

GO ON A NATURE WALK

Supplies: Bible, large blanket, snack, camera, backpack, hiking hat, stroller, sanitizer, "Allergy Alert" (printable resource, see page 2 for instructions)

- Place infants in a stroller and go on a walk outside.
- Talk about hiking at Breaker Rock Beach.
- Sit on a blanket in the shade and serve a snack to eat while hearing the Bible Story.
- Take photos of each child wearing the hiking hat and holding the backpack. Sanitize hat between uses.

EXTEND: Print the photos of the children and add to their Keepsake Books.

ROLL A VERSE

Supplies: "Theme Verse Strips" (pack item 31), "Juice Box Vehicles" (pack item 8), *VBS 2024 Theme Stickers* (9781430088820), clean oatmeal container, colored paper, clear contact plastic, Music for Babies–2s CD

- Cover the oatmeal container with colored paper. Decorate with "Theme Verse Strips" (pack item 31) and *VBS 2024 Theme Stickers* or copy vehicles from "Juice Box Vehicles" (pack item 8). Cover the container and decorations with clear contact plastic.
- Sit on the floor with a child. Help her hold the container and look at the stickers and verse strips.
- Point to each verse strip and read the verse.
- Show her how to roll the container on the floor. Sing "Sing to God a Thanksgiving Song" while rolling the container back and forth.

DAYS 1–5   BABIES–YOUNGER 1s • THEME ACTIVITIES

SPLASH IN WATER (OUTDOOR ACTIVITY)

Supplies: Toddler water table, towel, water source, Music for Babies–2s CD

- Provide a toddler water table with water.
- Hold the baby close enough to reach out and touch the water.
- Guide her to touch and splash the water.
- Say: "God has a plan for (insert child's name)" as the child plays in the water.
- Sing "Breaker Rock Beach" as water play continues.
- Supervise children closely while playing with water.

Leader Tip: If a water table is unavailable, use a watering can to pour water on the baby's hands or simply explore water coming from an indoor sink faucet.

ROCK A BABY DOLL

Supplies: Bible, "Bible Story Picture" (pack items 1–5), "Book: *Can You Find My Baby?*" (pack item 22), baby doll

- Sit in a rocking chair with an infant in your lap. Help her hold the baby doll and rock.
- Comment: "You are taking care of this baby. Your mama (or other grown-up) takes care of you."
- Read "Book: *Can You Find My Baby?*" (pack item 22).
- Open the Bible and share the Bible story. Show the Bible story picture and talk about how the child in the story was loved by his parents.
- Sing "I Love You" (Music and Movement Tab).

EXTEND: Help children match baby animals to their mamas on page 5 of the Keepsake Book.

DAYS 1–5

EXPLORE A FELT WALL

Supplies: "Felt Wall Instructions" (pack item 32); "Felt Wall Boulders" (pack item 19); "Felt Wall Pieces (pack item 20); "Magnifying Glasses" (pack item 13); blue, green, and brown felt purchased by the yard; variety of colors of felt; silk flowers and greenery; clean-release poster strips

- Prepare the felt wall as described in "Felt Wall Instructions" (pack item 32).
- Each day make a variety of new items available.
- Guide the children in adding the items to the wall.
- Talk to children about going to Breaker Rock Beach and what they might see.
- Show children how to look at the felt wall using "Magnifying Glasses" (pack item 13).
- Look for opportunities to add Bible story pictures, or other pack items to the wall, which will lead to Bible conversations.

Leader Tip: The felt wall is an activity for children to experience daily throughout VBS. Keep in mind, children this age will enjoy removing items as much as they enjoy putting them on the wall. They will enjoy the process more than the finished product.

MAKE TRAIL MIX

Supplies: Bible, "Bible Story Picture" (pack items 1–5), "Allergy Alert" (printable resource, see page 2 for instructions), bowls, small cups, scoops, fish-shaped crackers, bear-shaped crackers, candy-coated chocolate candy, other suitable trail mix items

- Post an allergy alert poster on the door prior to arrival. List all ingredients included in the trail mix.
- Pour each trail mix ingredient in a bowl, one ingredient per bowl, and set the bowls on the table with a scoop in each bowl.
- Invite a child to make trail mix with you. Assist her in washing her hands before starting.
- Show her how to scoop a small amount of each ingredient into her cup.
- Sit at the table and talk about Today's Point while she enjoys her snack. Use the "Bible Story Picture" (pack items 1–5) to talk about the story.

EXTEND: Guide children to follow the dotted line trail to the Bible on page 11 in their Keepsake Books.

DAYS 1–5

GO CAMPING AT BREAKER ROCK BEACH

Supplies: Bible, "Lanterns" (pack item 15), "Picnic Food" (pack item 18), "Book: *Let's Go Camping*" (pack item 23), "Flip-book: *Breaker Rock Beach*" (pack item 24), "Flip-book Assembly" (pack item 33), "Magnifying Glasses" (pack item 13), picnic basket, plastic food, tent, beach chair, beach towel

- Assemble the "Flip-book: *Breaker Rock Beach*" (pack item 24) according to the instructions on "Flip-book Assembly" (pack item 33).
- Set up the tent to create a campsite in a corner of the room. Place the books in the chair. Place the plastic food and "Picnic Food" (pack item 18) in the picnic basket. Add "Lanterns" (pack item 15) to the campsite.
- Join a child as he explores the campsite. Sit on the towel and talk about camping. Say: "Camping is fun. You can sleep in a tent and cook your food outside."
- Invite him to join you on the beach towel and read "Book: *Let's Go Camping*" (pack item 23).
- Open the Bible and pretend to use the magnifying glass to read the Bible story.
- Say a prayer thanking God for (child's name) and all he is learning at VBS.

DAYS 1–5

DECORATE A KITE

Supplies: *2024 VBS Theme Stickers* (9781430088820), white paper plates, scissors (leader use only), washable markers, yarn, hole punch, craft stick, tape

- Prior to the session, punch two holes in the outer edge of the paper plate approximately four inches apart. Cut the middle out of the paper plate. Cut yarn into four-foot lengths. Lay a plate, stickers, piece of yarn, craft stick, and markers on a tray.
- Allow a child to decorate the kite with markers and stickers. Help him thread one end of yarn through the top two holes and tie a knot. Assist him in taping the other end of the yarn to a craft stick and wrapping the yarn around the craft stick.
- Say: "People like to fly kites at the beach. We are having fun pretending we are at Breaker Rock Beach. We are also learning God has a plan for us."

EXTEND: Take the kite outside during outdoor playtime and show how to unwrap the yarn and hold the craft stick while running and flying the kite.

OLDER 1s–2s • THEME ACTIVITIES

MAKE TIDE POOL LIFE HANDPRINTS

Supplies: "Tide Pool Life Handprint Patterns" (pack item 34); washable red, orange, green, and brown paint; foam paintbrush; shallow pan; white paper; painting smock

- Place a painting smock on a child. Pour a small amount of paint in the shallow pan.
- Refer to "Tide Pool Life Handprint Patterns" (pack item 34) for handprint animal ideas.
- Use the foam brush to apply paint to the child's hand for handprints. Identify and describe the tide pool animals as you make handprints on white paper.
- Write the child's name and *VBS 2024* in one corner.
- Say a brief prayer thanking God for fun at VBS.

EXTEND: Make crab handprints on pages 12 and 13 of the Keepsake Book and fingerprint leaves in the trees on page 3.

DRIVE A BEACH VEHICLE

Supplies: Bible, "Bible Story Picture" (pack items 1–5), "Vehicle Wheel and Instructions" (pack item 29), "Vehicle Front" (pack item 30), cardboard box, painter's tape, Music for Babies–2s CD

- Follow the instructions on "Vehicle Wheel and Instructions" (pack item 29) for making a cardboard beach vehicle.
- Make a tape path around the room. Show the vehicle to a child and talk about driving it on rocky beaches.
- Help him step into the vehicle and pick it up using the cut outs on the side of the box.
- Encourage him to carry the box and pretend to drive around the room on the path.
- Meet him at the end of the path. Help him sit on the floor. Allow him to sit inside the box if he would like.
- Hand him the Bible story picture. Open the Bible to the story and share it in your own words.
- Sing "Sing to God a Thanksgiving Song."

DAYS 1–5

MATCH WATER BOTTLES AND LIDS

Supplies: "Theme Verse Strips" (pack item 31), colored paper, scissors, assortment of non-disposable water bottles with lids

- Copy the "Theme Verse Strips" (pack item 31) onto colored paper. Insert a verse strip in each water bottle and put on the lid. Place the bottles in a basket.
- Sit on the floor with a child and explore the different colors and sizes of water bottles. Ask if he has a water bottle at home.
- Talk about the places we might take a water bottle.
- Help him remove the lids and discover the verse strip inside. Read the verse each time he finds a strip. Say: "Thank You, God, for Jesus."
- Continue exploring the bottles by mixing up the lids and encouraging him to find the right lid for each bottle.

Leader Tip: Older twos will be able to match lids to four or five bottles while ones might need only two or three bottles. Remove or add bottles depending on the child's interest and ability. Do not use disposable water bottles.

PLAY IN SAND

Supplies: "Bible Story Picture" (pack items 1–5), "Sand Recipes" (pack item 25), ingredients for sand, sand pail and shovel, sensory table or tub, tape, "Allergy Alert" (printable resource, see page 2 for instructions)

- Prepare sand using one of the recipes. Keep a lid on the table or tub when a leader is not available to supervise this activity.
- Tape the Bible story picture on the wall next to the sensory table.
- Place a sand pail and shovel in the sand. Encourage a child to join you in playing with the sand.
- Comment: "If you go to the beach there is a lot of sand. The sand at Breaker Rock Beach might have little pebbles and rocks in it."
- Demonstrate how to use the shovel to scoop sand into the pail.
- Point to the Bible story picture and tell the story.
- Sing "This Is the Way" (Music and Movement Tab).
- Supervise children closely while playing with sand.

DAYS 1–5

OLDER 1s–2s • THEME ACTIVITIES

GO ON A HIKE

Supplies: Bible, "Book: *Can You Find My Baby?*" (pack item 22), hiking boots or rain boots, hat, sunglasses, jacket or vest, binoculars

- Lay the hiking clothes on a mat and allow a child to begin to explore the clothes.
- Assist her in dressing up like she is going on a hike. Say: "You would need boots to hike at Breaker Rock Beach, and you might need to wear a jacket."
- Talk about all the things she might see on her hike. Suggest there might be mama animals with their babies.
- Sit on the floor and read "Book: Can You *Find My Baby?*" (pack item 22).
- Remind her that in our Bible stories this week we heard about several children like David, Samuel, and Jesus who had families who loved them.
- Say: "Thank You, God, for families and thank You, God, for Jesus."
- Encourage her to take the binoculars and go for a walk around the room.

EXTEND: Help children match baby animals to their mamas on page 5 of the Keepsake Book. Take pictures of children in hiking clothes and add to the Keepsake Books.

MATCH ANIMALS TO THEIR SHADOWS

Supplies: "Animals" (pack item 16), "Animal Shadows" (pack item 17), toy sea life animals, Music for Babies–2s CD

- Allow a child to explore the sea life animals.
- While the child is playing, invite another child to play a matching game.
- Pick up one of the "Animals" (pack item 16) and show him how to match it to a shadow.
- Assist the child in matching the other animals.
- Encourage the children to take turns matching animals and exploring the sea life animals.
- Sing "Church" as children play with animals.

DAYS 1–5

DRIVE ON A TRAIL

Supplies: Bible, "Juice Box Vehicles" (pack item 8), "Juice Box Vehicle Instructions" (pack item 27), "Vehicle Trail" (pack item 35), four empty juice boxes, double-sided tape, painter's tape, sand and pebbles, clear contact plastic, plastic trees or greenery

- Follow "Juice Box Vehicle Instructions" (pack item 27) for making juice box vehicles.
- Lay the "Vehicle Trail" (pack item 35) on a low table and tape around all edges. Scatter a few pebbles and sand on the trail. Cover the pebbles and sand with clear contact plastic.
- Invite a child to move the vehicles along the trail. Talk about how bumpy it would be to drive on a trail covered in sand and pebbles.
- Sit close by while the child plays; open the Bible and tell the Bible story.
- Comment: "God loved (name person in story), and He loves you and has a plan for you." Encourage him to say: "God has a plan for me."

DISCOVER PICTURES IN BOX LIDS

Supplies: "Animal Match" (pack item 9), six cardboard jewelry boxes with lids, double-sided tape, tray, *2024 VBS Logo Stickers* (9781430088257)

- Tape the bottom of each box to the tray. Choose five animal cards and place one in each box on the tray. Place a VBS logo sticker in one box.
- Tape each animal matching card and a logo sticker to the inside of a lid. Place the box lids in a basket next to the tray.
- Show a child the animals in the boxes. Say: "Can you find the raccoon? Where is the bear?"
- Set the basket of lids in front of him. Pull a lid from the basket and point out the picture inside the lid.
- Say: "Here is a bear. This lid belongs on the box with the bear inside." Place the lid on the appropriate box.
- Encourage him to remove a lid from the basket and find the matching box. Continue until all boxes are covered.

EXTEND: Older twos will enjoy playing a memory game. When all the lids are on the boxes, name an animal and ask the child if he remembers which box the animal is in.

1s AND 2s LOVE TO MOVE AND THEY LOVE MUSIC.

Music and movement can be used to teach, to comfort or stimulate a child, and to encourage group participation. Try these ideas for incorporating music and movement into the VBS session:

- Sing or play music and move around the room with an upset child.
- Play musical instruments while waiting for a turn or while waiting for parents.
- March to music to burn energy before a quiet activity. Challenge older 2s and younger 3s to play a simple musical instrument while marching. (Note: This is a difficult skill for most 1s and 2s.)
- Use songs to help teach and reinforce Bible truths.
- Use music in place of conversation. Example: Don't just say the Bible verse, sing it instead!
- Play music quietly in the background as children play.
- Wave fabric streamers to music while leading children to move around the room.
- Play calming music quietly during nap or rest times. Sing simple songs to familiar tunes such as "Mary Had a Little Lamb" (see reverse side).

MUSIC & MOVEMENT

BIBLE-TEACHING SONGS AND ACTIVITY SONG

I LOVE YOU

Tune: *"Are You Sleeping"*

Baby bear, baby bear,
I love you; I love you.
I love you baby bear,
I love you baby bear,
Yes, I do, yes, I do.
*Substitute: baby sea lion,
baby owl, baby wolf*

THIS IS THE WAY

Tune: *"Here We Go 'Round the Mulberry Bush"*

This is the way we dig, dig, dig.
Dig, dig, dig,
Dig, dig, dig.
This is the way we dig, dig, dig,
When we go to the beach.
Substitute fish, hike, swim

THANK YOU, GOD

Tune: *"Mary Had a Little Lamb"*

Thank You, God for Jesus,
Jesus, Jesus.
Thank You, God for Jesus
Because He loves me so.

GOD HAS A PLAN FOR ME

Tune: *"Mary Had a Little Lamb"*

God, You have a plan for me,
Plan for me, plan for me.
God, You have a plan for me.
You have a plan for me.

JESUS, JESUS, HE LOVES ME

Clap and Chant

Jesus, Jesus, He loves me.
He loves me.
He loves me.
Jesus, Jesus, He loves me.

Repeat the chant: slower, faster, louder, softer

BREAKER ROCK BEACH

Take a walk along the coast
Sand beneath your toes
Take it all in, come on let's go
Breaker Rock Beach

See the tall majestic pines
Endless shorelines
Never know what you're gonna find
Breaker Rock Beach

There is a rock
That stands the test of time
Where the wind and waters rise
And waves are always breakin'
There is a rock
Where we can build our lives
His name is Jesus Christ
And we will not be shaken ... at Breaker Rock Beach

When you're tempted and you're tried
By the storms of life
There's a place that you can hide
Breaker Rock Beach

In a world of shifting sand
On Christ we stand
He's the only perfect plan
Breaker Rock Beach

REPEAT CHORUS

Do not be conformed to this age
But be transformed by the renewing of your mind
So that you may discern
What is the good, pleasing, and perfect will of God

REPEAT CHORUS

Breaker Rock Beach
Breaker Rock Beach

Words and music by Paul Marino and Jeremy Johnson. Arranged by Paul Marino and Jeremy Johnson. © Copyright 2023 Van Ness Press, Inc. (ASCAP) (admin. by Lifeway Worship c/o Music Services, www.musicservices.org). All rights reserved. Used by permission. CCLI #7218857.

SING TO GOD A THANKSGIVING SONG

Sing to God a Thanksgiving song
Sing to God a Thanksgiving song
Sing to God a Thanksgiving song
Sing, sing, sing

Words and music by Kevin Lintz.
© Copyright 1998 Broadman Press (SESAC) (admin by Music Services,
www.musicservices.org). All rights reserved. Used by permission. CCLI #4582052.

CHURCH

Church, church, we love to go to church
Church, church, we love to go to church
*Our teachers tell us stories from the Bible
We love to go to church

*Substitute: We learn how we should all love
one another; We see our friends and sing and
pray together.

Words and music by Janet McMahan.
© Copyright 2004 Van Ness Press, Inc. (ASCAP) (admin. by Music Services,
www.musicservices.org). All rights reserved. Used by permission. CCLI #4579728.

JESUS IS BORN

God sent Jesus to the earth
He was placed in a manger

Shepherds came and angels sang
Jesus is born
Mary, Joseph held Him tight
On that peaceful starry night
God sent Him to bring us life
Jesus is born

God sent Jesus to the earth
He was placed in a manger
Shepherds came and angels sang
Jesus is born
Mary, Joseph held Him tight
On that peaceful starry night
God sent Him to bring us life
Jesus is born

God sent Jesus to the earth
He was placed in a manger
Shepherds came and angels sang
Jesus is born
Mary, Joseph held Him tight
On that peaceful starry night
God sent Him to bring us life
Jesus is born
Jesus is born

Words and music by Paul Marino and Jeremy Johnson.
© Copyright 2020 Van Ness Press, Inc. (ASCAP) (admin. by Lifeway Worship c/o
Music Services, www.musicservices.org). All rights reserved. Used by permission.
CCLI #7151014.

JESUS LOVES YOU AND ME

Jesus loves you and me
Jesus loves you and me
He loves my family and my friends
Jesus loves you and me

Words and music by Esther Maus-Tester. © Copyright 2010 McKinney Music (BMI) (admin. by Lifeway Worship). All rights reserved. Used by permission. CCLI #5651937.

I CAN LEARN ABOUT GOD'S LOVE

*I can learn about God's love at home, at church, at play.
Jesus taught about God's care, we thank Him ev'ry day.

*Substitute: child's name

Words by Joyce Wood Capps. Music by Dora Ann Purdy. © Copyright 2002 Broadman Press (SESAC) (admin. by Music Services). All rights reserved. Used by permission. CCLI #4451499.

JESUS TAUGHT

Jesus taught, Jesus taught people everywhere
Jesus taught, Jesus taught people everywhere
He helped them learn about God
He helped them learn about God
Jesus taught, Jesus taught people everywhere
Jesus taught, Jesus taught people everywhere

Words and music by Esther Maus-Tester. © Copyright 2011 McKinney Music, Inc. (BMI) (admin. by Lifeway Worship c/o Music Services, www.musicservices.org). All rights reserved. Used by permission. CCLI #6014906.

MUSIC AND MOVEMENT

LEARN ABOUT GOD

Learn about God (Learn about God)
Choose to obey Him (Choose to obey Him)
Learn about God (Learn about God)
Choose to obey Him (Choose to obey Him)
Learn about God
Choose to obey Him

Open up the Bible
It's the Word of God
It tells us how to live like Jesus
Every word is true
It's up to me and you to

Repeat Chorus

Open up the Bible
It's the Word of God
It tells us how to live like Jesus
Every word is true
It's up to me and you to

Repeat Chorus

Learn about God
Choose to obey Him

Words and music by Paul Marino and Jeremy Johnson.
Arranged by Paul Marino and Jeremy Johnson.
© Copyright 2023 Van Ness Press, Inc. (ASCAP) (admin. by Lifeway Worship c/o Music Services, www.musicservices.org). All rights reserved. Used by permission. CCLI #7218862.